A Cry From The Wild

A Tale Of Two Orphans

Lissa Ruben

BCA

LONDON · NEW YORK · SYDNEY · TORONTO

A Macdonald Book

First published in Great Britain in 1991 by
Macdonald & Co (Publishers) Ltd

This edition published in 1991 by
BCA by arrangement with
Macdonald & Co (Publishers) Ltd

Designed by Barney Wan

CN 4074

Phototypeset by Wyvern Typesetting Limited, Bristol

Printed and bound in Hong Kong. Produced by Mandarin

Macdonald & Co (Publishers) Ltd
165 Great Dover Street
London SE1 4YA

A member of Maxwell Macmillan Pergamon Publishing Corporation

DEDICATION

To a very special family

My parents, Monty and Hilary, and my sister, Mandy.

With much, much love and gratitude.

ACKNOWLEDGEMENTS

Kenya: I would not be writing these acknowledgements at all if it wasn't for my great friends, Jill Woodley and her mother, Daphne Sheldrick (MBE), without whom the orphans would have no future and of course this book would not have been possible.

The keepers, for their love and devotion to the orphans: Atanash Mwendo Mulei, Erastus Baraza Kagoi, Dennis Mutongoi Ndolo, Francis Ndambuki, Jackson Nyerere Nzau, John Ilui, John Mbulu, Joseph Lugoma Muhaya, Joseph Munguti Chambi, Enos Okode, Kioko Mutua, Mishak Nzimbi, Moses Alingo Oluga, Muendo Nzimbi, Nyaga Nthiga Zakariah, Peter Mutuku Muinde; and Grace Wayua, Johnston Maweu Itumo, Peter Isika, who work at the house and inevitably find themselves caught up with elephants, too. A big thank you to all the volunteers who give so much of their time: Doris Zola, a friend and stalwart from the very beginning, who will go to any lengths for the elephants; together with 'Abo' Abbonizio, Susie and Anthony Ray, Adam Tweedy, Dave Wade, Frank and Majorie Watts, and the many others. Deepest thanks to Dieter and Ushi Rottcher, who never let us down.

Sincere appreciation to Dr Richard Leakey, Director, Kenya Wildlife Services; the former Deputy Director, Joseph Mburugu; Senior Warden of Tsavo East, Stephen Gichangi; and Joe Kioko, former Senior Warden of Tsavo East and now Deputy Director, Kenya Wildlife Services, in charge of National Parks; for their continuing battle to save our elephants together with the rest of Kenya's wildlife.

Special thanks to Fiona Alexander; Colour Centre – Mehmood Quairshy, who has always taken such care and a personal interest in my photography, together with Salma and Farzana and the rest of the staff; to true friends, Simon Trevor in Tsavo East, Bill and Ruth Woodley in Tsavo West, for their friendship and for sharing their homes with me on my numerous trips to Tsavo over the years, and for all their collective work in their tireless fight for conservation. And Nan Baillie, who has been part of the family for so many years; Elijah, who works for my parents; and Gary Walder, a quiet pillar of strength.

My parents – Monty, for your mountains of love and support, not just for me, but also for the elephants, and Hilary, too, together with your many suggestions and invaluable advice in the writing of this book; and my sister, Mandy, who, with my queries and doubts, together with her fine editing, gave me real courage and support, particularly when I realized my deadline was almost upon me.
And in memory of a remarkable sheep, Boozie, who died last year.

England: Thank you to my agent, Toby Eady, who never doubted this project from the beginning. Gary Hodges, wildlife artist, for his friendship and very special drawing on the title page and page 4, and his photographs/E.I.A. for the Introduction: bottom page 11, top page 12, and bottom pages 14 and 15. Also, Elefriends, for their photograph, top page 13. The *Daily Mail* for the courtesy of their photograph for the inside back cover flap. The David Shepherd Conservation Foundation whose three months sponsorship enabled me to continue, I am most grateful. Ian Redmond for his interest and advice, Wyeth Laboratories who have donated every bag of SMA Goldcap needed to raise the orphans, and to British Airways for flying it out.

Barney Wan, who designed this book for me, and together with his exceptional talent and sensitivity, makes him such a wonderful person to work with, and who is also a good friend. And Nick Webb, my publisher – for all his time and support. Thank you.

So much appreciation goes to the dedication of the following special people/organizations and their teams for their endless work in fighting for conservation and for striving to give all animals a better quality of life:

Care for the Wild – Bill Jordan: 1 Ashfolds, Horsham Road, Rusper, West Sussex RH12 4QX.

Elefriends – Will Travers: Cherrytree Cottage, Coldharbour, Dorking, Surrey RH5 6HA.

Environmental Investigation Agency – Dave Currey: 208–209 Upper Street, London N1 1RL.

The African Ele-Fund – Ian Redmond: P.O. Box 308, Bristol BS99 7LQ.

The David Sheldrick Wildlife Trust – Daphne Sheldrick: P.O. Box 15555, Nairobi, Kenya.

Zoo Check – Virginia McKenna & Bill Travers: Cherrytree Cottage, Coldharbour, Dorking, Surrey RH5 6HA.

Also, to all the other individuals and organizations that are battling for conservation, too.

Part of the royalties from this book
will be donated to
The David Sheldrick Wildlife Trust.

Lissa Ruben

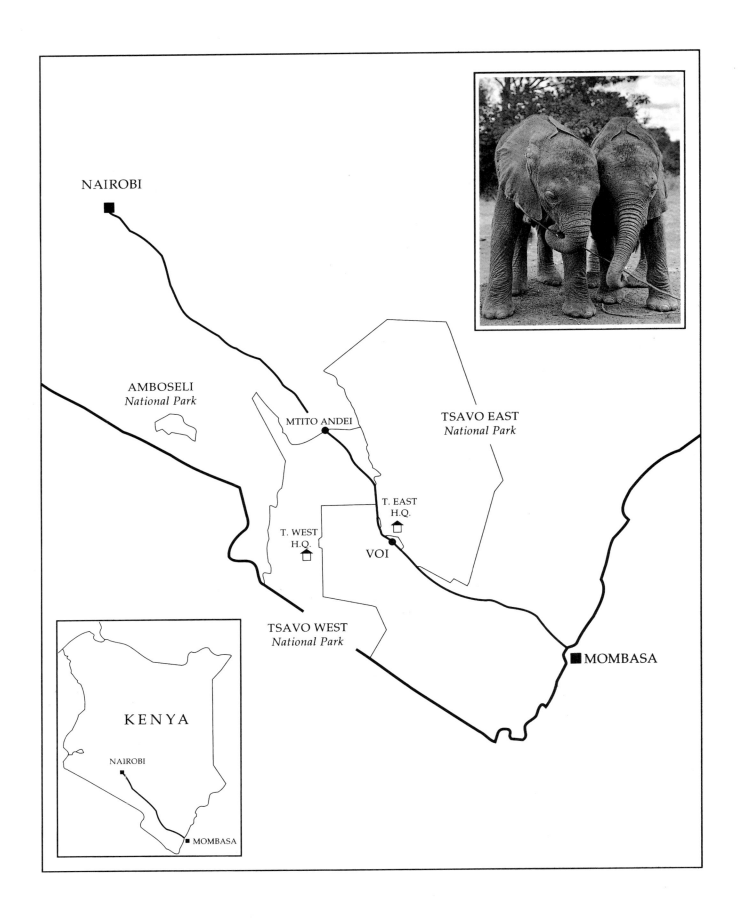

NAIROBI

AMBOSELI
National Park

MTITO ANDEI

TSAVO EAST
National Park

T. EAST
H.Q.

T. WEST
H.Q.

VOI

TSAVO WEST
National Park

MOMBASA

KENYA

NAIROBI

MOMBASA

INTRODUCTION

My story is about two small elephants—two in particular that witnessed the massacre of their herd as a result of Man's insatiable lust for ivory. However, first I must tell you just a little about this very special part of the world.

Overlooking the Athi Plains, in Nairobi National Park, stands a small wooden house—Daphne Sheldrick's home—and a sanctuary for orphaned animals. It is hard to believe that this haven exists barely half an hour from the increasing turmoil and bustle of the metropolis. I love the short dirt track that wends its way up to the house. Giraffes browse peacefully, elands frequent the grasslands, impalas and zebras are in abundance, too, for there is no fence between the house and the wild animals in the Park.

I immediately feel nature's magic at work and the pressures of the city fade into oblivion. As one rounds the final corner, there is an amazing flash of colour from the rock garden—a paradise for the sunbirds; warthogs visit daily, and after their treat of grain, enjoy the warmth of the brown earth and the peace that prevails.

Daphne was born and brought up in Kenya. She married David Sheldrick and they lived for twenty-eight years in Tsavo East National Park—an area of 5,000 square miles. Gazetted in

1948, David devoted his life to the Park's development—a perfect ecosystem so rich in wildlife. At the end of 1976 he was transferred to Nairobi. Tragically, David died six months later of a heart attack. Daphne was given special permission to build her house in the Park and she immediately formed The David Sheldrick Wildlife Trust in his memory. This was also to enable her to continue her commitment to conservation.

Together with her daughter Jill, Daphne not only raises orphaned animals but dedicates much time to other important projects such as providing money for both the preservation of the black rhino, and the fight against poaching, with an emphasis on the protection of elephants; offering assistance to other needy animals and providing educational articles, lectures on wildlife and training in wildlife management, all of which are so vital if our natural heritage is to be preserved.

In her Tsavo years, many an orphan was brought to Daphne and she raised just about every species of animal, the majority of which returned successfully to the wild. Elephants were the most problematical and all those below the age of one year died. The prime reason for this was the fact that they are totally dependent on milk during this period, although they do start eating greens towards the end of their first twelve months. For years Daphne tried to find the right milk formula and after much trial, error and heartache, she discovered the solution in SMA Goldcap—a soya bean-based powder used for premature and weak infants. Her discovery followed the

crucial realization that young elephants are unable to digest the fat in cow's milk.

In 1986 the first orphan arrived in Daphne's Nairobi home — a rhino named Sam, all of six weeks old. His mother had been unsuccessful in fending off lions and rangers had rescued him from certain death. He was badly mauled, but soon responded to treatment, together with Daphne's loving care and the help of a very special sheep called Boozie, who was to be his constant companion. Rhinos need constant company to replace that of their mother and Boozie obviously loved Sam as much as he did her. Baby rhinos look somewhat stumpy and I will always remember this small, compact bundle bounding and bouncing after the delights of a mudwallow.

The next arrival was Olmeg, a tiny elephant, a mere three weeks old and a victim of poaching. He was in a terrible condition and his little ears were burnt to a crisp. In the wild calves are protected from the elements by the shelter of their mothers' bodies and the rest of the herd. Olmeg was the youngest infant elephant to be raised in captivity and Daphne knew she had definitely won.

So started the line of orphaned elephants in Nairobi, as the world's greed for ivory grew.

How many of us have witnessed the sensitivity of these great and gentle beasts, their compassion and intelligence, or know of their complex social structure? After a twenty-two-month gestation period, they are born into a world of love and reassurance, surrounded by a family of aunts, brothers and sisters, and a mum who is never far away. To ensure survival, tutoring begins early, for there is much to learn; generations of accumulated knowledge surround their search for food and water. The elephant's digestive system is inefficient, only

digesting forty per cent of what is eaten. Therefore, they spend much time in a day eating—an adult eats for approximately eighteen to twenty hours out of twenty-four, sleeping for between three and four hours in that period. The younger calves need to sleep more and a good opportunity for this is provided in the heat of the day, when everyone stops under a large shady tree for temporary relief from the sun, and, of course, at night.

The females bond together for life, led by the matriarch, who is totally responsible for the well-being of the herd, respected by all and whose position is never disputed. I have often watched herds of elephants and it is amazing how they might all freeze at exactly the same time as some signal or sound, inaudible to human ears, is transmitted. No one will move until the matriarch does. Tragically these days, especially in Tsavo, there are very few large herds to be found, only many splintered groups in small numbers. If the matriarch has been killed, they are leaderless until another old female takes over. With no leader they are nervous and confused and travel without direction. Cows can breed from the age of twelve, producing a calf every four to five years.

The bulls reach puberty around twelve, when they leave the herd and spend their teenage years romping and roaming the grasslands, joining up with more mature bulls to continue

their tutelage. Bulls are capable of fertilizing a female at this age, but are not big enough to compete with older bulls until they are into their mid-twenties. However, only those over thirty come into musth – a period of aggressive behaviour when a male challenges others in the bull herd to improve his status – and it is in this condition that they are preferred by the females.

An elephant's death is surrounded by much mysticism. At the time of death, trunks gently touch and probe the carcass and attempts are made to lift it. It is not until they are completely satisfied that the life force has departed, will they leave. After the flesh has decomposed, elephants are known to remove the tusks and carry them some way off before eventually discarding them. Sometimes they smash the tusks against rocks, splintering them into many pieces. It seems elephants know just how special their ivory is. Sometimes the herd will bury their dead, covering them with soil and vegetation. Elephants may bury other dead animals too. On passing a skeleton of old they often stop and silently touch the bones, perhaps recognizing a friend of months gone by.

There has been much controversy over the destruction caused to the habitat by the elephant, especially in Tsavo. However, amongst other things, elephants are, without doubt, invaluable in opening up spaces where bush has become very thick and they help all sorts of plants and trees to germinate as the seeds are deposited in their dung. They also enhance other species' chances of survival.

For example, during a drought they pull down more trees and branches than they can eat themselves, thus bringing the foliage into the reach of other game. They also possess a unique knowledge, which they demonstrate on returning to dry sand river beds to dig for water. Using their tusks and trunks they dig and, together with the soles of their feet, they reach down to the water-table making a water-hole. Other animals are then quick to come and quench their thirsts.

By saving the elephant we are saving our environment, too, for they go hand in hand. Who knows how disastrous it would be if we were to lose these remarkable animals?

There is nothing more magical than sitting and watching these magnificent animals. On the move, they make their way in uncanny silence. The tiny calves tumble along, little bundles of joy, still undecided as to what a trunk is all about — totally uncoordinated as it flops from side to side, gets tripped over, trodden on and even sucked like a thumb. Their excitement and delight on reaching a water-hole is unforgettable, as thirsts are quenched, followed by a wallow. Games are played and everyone joins in with abandon.

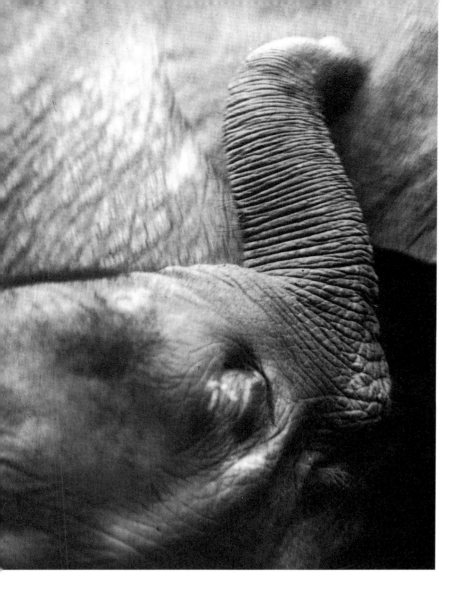

There is a tale that, for me, demonstrates one of the many wonders of the elephant. One day scientists studying elephants came upon two with a buffalo between them. They never left the side of this animal and were constantly reassuring and comforting it as they slowly wended their way. It wasn't until some time later that the scientists realized the buffalo was blind. . . .

I can't help thinking that surely if people knew more about these extraordinary animals, they wouldn't buy ivory. It is this lack of knowledge that inspired this book, which I hope will help the world to understand why 'only elephants should wear ivory'.

CHAPTER ONE

NDUME—The thinking Eli. Always chewing on something, seemingly in his own little world, almost as if puffing on a pipe, a thousand thoughts away. So content in his eight months of wisdom—*now*.

MALAIKA—Swahili for angel, and her face is just that. So refined and so gentle. Her skin texture so smooth around her fat healthy cheeks. Her sparkling eyes full of naughty ideas—*now*.

But let's go back a few months. Emergency: two tiny orphans need rescuing, an hour's plane-ride from Nairobi. But how small? In what condition? We know so little except that time is crucial. They will be dehydrated and stressed and Meru is hot. Every moment is precious if they are to survive. There is so much to be done. Dieter, our vet, must be contacted, an aeroplane hired, transport provided to meet them off the plane, stable-room arranged.

The house is a bustle of activity as preparations get under way. It's too late to leave today. Morning finally arrives. Bottles, teats, milk-powder, water, blankets—the list continues to grow. Finally we all meet at Wilson—Africa's busiest light aircraft airport. Most of the seats are being removed from a twin otter. Dieter, two keepers—John and Peter—and myself are to fly up. Also present is our Assistant Director for National Parks, Mr Mburugu (who will remain in Meru), Simon Trevor and his assistant, Barbara Tyack, who will film the rescue. Jill, as always, checks nothing is missing, a mistake can be a loss. She will remain, await our arrival, and, in the interim, will continue preparations at base.

At last we're off. It's Peter's and John's first flight. They sit clutching each other's knees, a mixture of sheer terror, excitement and expectation on their faces.

We reach Meru National Park, barren, dry, void of game. We fly over a mass of elephant bones—I try not to think of the suffering as herds are mowed down, small calves left to die as tusks are hacked from their mothers' bodies.

Malaika and Ndume find solace together.

Standing in the back are two tiny elephants.

We land—not a vehicle in sight. Are we too late? The minutes tick by; we wait silently. And then quite suddenly, the clouds of red dust appear in the distance. I hold my breath. As they get closer, we see only a Toyota Landcruiser. It pulls to a stop and a group of park rangers clamber out. Mr Mburugu is impatient. What's going on? Where are they? We are assured the truck is close behind. Again we wait. More billowing dust rises and this time it is the truck. Rattling and dilapidated, it eventually pulls up beside us.

Standing in the back are two tiny elephants.

They look so small, so lost, so fragile. I can't wait to climb onto the back. As the temperature soars, minutes become vital, each moment critical to their survival. They are dehydrated and we must work fast. Despite their horrendous ordeal, they still have some strength. Dieter decides to give them a small amount of tranquilizer. The little female remains standing, but the male collapses. As quickly as possible we place his tiny body onto a tarpaulin and carry him to the plane. Then we do the same with the female.

A crowd of Africans gather from nowhere, jostling with each other for a peep into the plane. The heat is now unbearable. We must take off. At long last the doors are closed and we are airborne. If I thought the journey out was endless, the one homeward becomes almost intolerable.

I often catch Dieter's eye. There is nothing to be said, so little we can do. We spray them with water, keeping Ndume's ear flapping to try and cool his body. Elephants' ears are a very efficient cooling system—as they flap the blood travelling through the large veins behind the ears is cooled; it then goes back into the body very much cooler than before. The images remain vivid—and Peter and John, lost in concern for those two tiny orphans, have almost forgotten their fear of flying.

Ndume seems to be sinking further and further away from us, his eyes receding deeper and deeper into their sockets. Malaika isn't looking too good either.

At long last we are back in Nairobi. The doors open—I can't believe the sea of faces, the surge of people. But I focus on only one—Jill. I am very relieved to see her standing there, her face full of anxiety and hope. I remember saying: 'It's okay. We've got them, a little boy and a little girl.'

Jill has the transport backed up. I can appreciate people's curiosity, but they are slowing us down. If only they could understand how vital every second is becoming. Dieter makes a hasty exit in order to get ahead. Malaika comes off first, then Ndume. Once again we carry this virtually lifeless form and I wonder: can he really make it?

Simon films as Dieter takes care of Ndume who seems to be sinking further and further away from us.

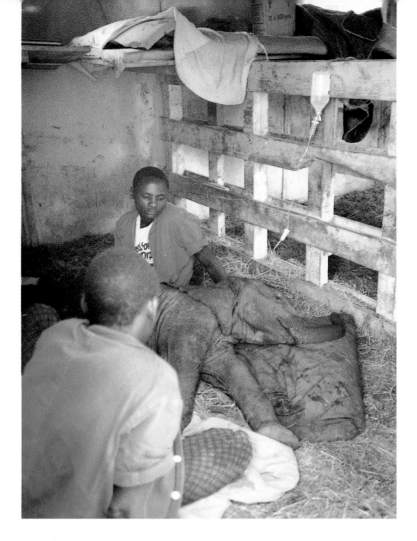

Peter (LEFT) and John anxiously wait as Ndume continues on the drip.

And then to the last leg home. Peter, John and I sit in the back of the van, doors tied open. We are escorted by people eager to help. Jill catches my eye—*yes* we must go faster. She pulls out and relays this urgent message to our driver.

Finally home and in to stables. As Malaika manages a few mouthfuls of milk from Daphne, Dieter puts Ndume on a drip. Malaika then sinks next-door, exhausted. She has a very bad gash on her back leg, which needs suturing. She is so tired, she doesn't even stir as Dieter works away.

We then turn Ndume onto his other side and continue the drip: once again we wait.

And then a miracle occurs—an answer to our prayers. Ndume slowly starts to stir and come round. It is getting late and we have to move him, put him in a room of his own: he is occupying someone else's and this can't be. There simply isn't one spare. We put him in one of the keeper's rooms, who is on leave—it is all we have.

Malaika takes a little more milk, she seems strangely calm, unnervingly so. Ndume's wobbly little legs, with our help, make their way to the new abode a few yards away. Not long after, he starts showing signs of trauma and stress which grow and grow. How much more can this

Ndume (TOP) and Malaika looked so very sick it was hard to believe they would ever survive.

Kioko (LEFT), Malaika, Jackson and Ndume go for a gentle walk in the early morning.

frail elephant take? As the nightmares flood back he becomes frantic. He wants his mother and he battles to get out of his strange confinement. We can't let him out into the cold, dark night. We feel so utterly helpless. He is screaming, trying to climb the walls, his trunk anxiously pushing through the window. It is agonizing for us all.

As Malaika sleeps Ndume battles. At long last dawn breaks: perhaps now he will calm down. We let them out of their stables. They greet each other—their little trunks elongating as they join together, intermingling so gently, so reassuringly, a touching moment we will witness each day.

Feeding is always a problem to begin with and of great concern to us. They lose whatever condition they may have fast and force feeding is not worth considering. Either they take to their bottle—which may take a lot of patience and subtle persuasion—or they die. The previous orphans had eventually taken to their 'tent', which Daphne and Jill discovered by accident after the arrival of Olmeg. To give Olmeg's badly sunburnt ears a chance of recovery they put up a fly, and it was under this canvas, resembling the bulk of his mother's body, that he started to respond. From then on the keeper would be on one side of the canvas offering the bottle underneath, with Olmeg on the other and the feeding problems were over. However, Ndume and Malaika were not to follow suit. As well as all the other problems, we had to try and make them interested in their bottles. Ndume wouldn't stop the desperate search for his mother either. Any movement in the bushes, be it the wind or a warthog, he'd go tumbling off as fast as his little legs would allow. You could feel his hope, desperation and disappointment. One ankle was badly sprained and although we knew too much rushing around was not good for it, to try and restrain him was certainly no alternative. Besides, if his broken heart healed, we felt sure his foot would, too.

It wasn't long before they discovered the warthogs on their routine visit each morning. As Malaika's appetite and strength grew, so did her interest. Off she'd run, trunk flopping from side to side. Then she'd slow down, take a few paces forward, a few back, fan her ears and muster a 'charge'. Needless to say, she wouldn't follow it through, but it seemed a wonderful game just the same. Sadly, this didn't seem to make Ndume any better. We did move him to a new stable, which met with his approval, as did the ever loyal, loving Boozie. What a wonderful sheep. She always seemed to be there for those who needed her most: after Sam she kept Dika company and now Ndume. He got such great comfort suckling her ear or softly touching her fat, warm belly with his tender trunk that Boozie moved into his stable. As his dementia gradually lessened, although still a very sad elephant, he was slowly beginning to improve.

It wasn't long before they discovered the warthogs on their routine visit every morning.

The milk round became more and more frantic—as did Jill and I. We were feeding them on demand to begin with and life became a constant round of weighing, mixing, heating, feeding and bottle-washing. In addition to the day's work, we were alternating night duty, too. As if this wasn't enough, we also had to find and train extra keepers.

As the elephants' plight became headline news, journalists pitched up daily at Daphne's. The mail poured in: she never stopped either. If she wasn't taken up with interviews, she was trying to keep abreast of the many wonderful letters and donations.

It was all so worthwhile; and as Ndume showed more and more signs of wanting to live, we began to feel we were winning at last.

Ndume got such great comfort touching Boozie's fat, warm body with his tender trunk.

Ndume (LEFT) and Malaika – trunks intermingling, so gently, so reassuringly.

Peter (LEFT) and Mishak bundle Ndume in blankets.

CHAPTER TWO

Nairobi, at 5,500 feet, can be very cold in the early morning. After the 6.00 a.m. feed, as the keepers bundled their charges in blankets—for without the warmth of their mothers' bodies this was a necessity—we would make the tea. In the early days, whether on night duty or not, Jill and I would share these moments with the keepers and the two orphans.

We kept a log of how much each elephant consumed over a twenty-four-hour period and as these totals began to climb, our anxiety would cautiously lessen. Eight to ten pints in the beginning was an average but very shaky start and not nearly enough: fifteen a day was what it should have started off at, rapidly rising to twenty. After the harrowing first two weeks, Malaika needed no encouragement, but Ndume remained low and worryingly inconsistent. We would discuss all this, how everybody's night had been and what the strategy would be for that particular day.

Every orphan is different, each with their own distinct personality, likes and dislikes (especially where the temperature of the milk is concerned!). Thus, there is no set formula. Some may be able to take a stronger milk solution than others; some may require preliminary feeding more constantly than others; most teeter on the brink. The younger they are the better it is. They have less to remember or less to forget and, consequently, settle down more easily. It never ceases to amaze me how strong they can be, although weighing approximately 100 kilos at birth could have something to do with it.

On Ndume's second night, as he continued to struggle, we could stand it no longer and decided to let him out. This turned out to be of no help at all, and trying to get him back inside was something we weren't prepared for. It took four of us what felt like an eternity to move him a mere twenty yards back to his stable.

OVERLEAF: Ndume desperate for his mother even tries suckling Malaika. Such sad, gaunt faces, cheekbones protruding.

The keepers help the orphans to find the will to live.

As important as the feeding is the elephants' will to live. They grieve so, a deep depression sets in and somehow we have to give them that will to live, to make them feel that life really is worth it after all. In doing this we have to be happy around them: being very sensitive they feel all our emotions. The keepers are particularly good with the orphans, their love consoles them. In the wild, baby elephants are never alone but are surrounded by a family unit of all ages and sizes, with the constant reassurance of their mothers, aunts, cousins, sisters and brothers. Now we have to try and give them this security. Consequently, every orphan has to have a keeper sleep alongside them in the straw at night. There is no question of the keeper sneaking out either, for the elephants check every so often, opening an eye to make quite sure their companion is still there. In addition, Ndume had nightmares for quite a while and would wake up in the night needing plenty of reassurance. It didn't take them long to discover the joys of being tucked up either. They would literally choose their spot, sink down, lie on their side and wait. The keeper would then place a canvas cushion under their heads, shift their legs into the most comfortable position and finally tuck them up with one blanket, if not two. Here they would remain for close to three hours until it was time for another bottle. Then the tucking up procedure would take place all over again!

Boozie, as always, appears when she is needed, but draws the line at getting into the tube.

OVERLEAF: We did introduce them to the others almost immediately.

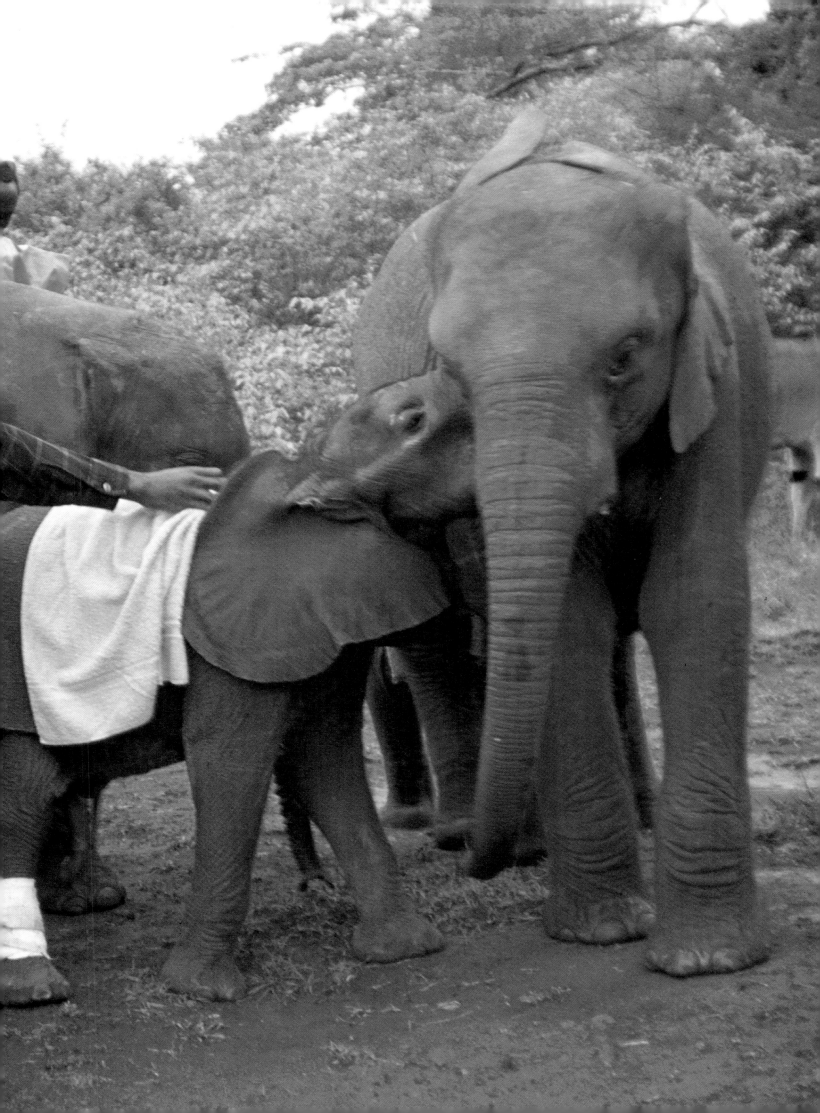

Apart from a brief moment with Taru, Malaika showed little interest in the others.

We did introduce them to the other elephants almost immediately. Malaika seemed quite content to fiddle around nearby; Ndume just wanted to nuzzle and suckle anyone who would let him. Bearing in mind that the rest of the entourage were only babies themselves, there was no reason why they should tolerate Ndume's little trunk pushing and probing for comfort. Nevertheless, Olmeg seemed to recognize his despair and awarded Ndume this privilege. However, as the company of the other three didn't seem to make much difference to the spirits of our recent arrivals and as Ndume and Malaika had to conserve the little

FACING: Ndume just wanted to suckle and nuzzle anyone who would let him, he pushes his way in between Dika and Olmeg.

Olmeg seems to recognize Ndume's despair and allows him to nuzzle.

strength they had, we decided it was better all round if they stayed closer to the house. This way we could monitor them and give them those bottles on demand, for they hated to be kept waiting. Also, Olmeg and Taru in particular needed plenty of exercise and varied vegetation, and the keepers had to take them quite a long way off for this. Dika, however, was still on four-hourly feeds, and came back to the house for these. His reaction when he learnt that the newcomers were permanent fixtures was something we hadn't counted on. He showed signs of intense jealousy, and when Ndume bellowed he became even more frantic.

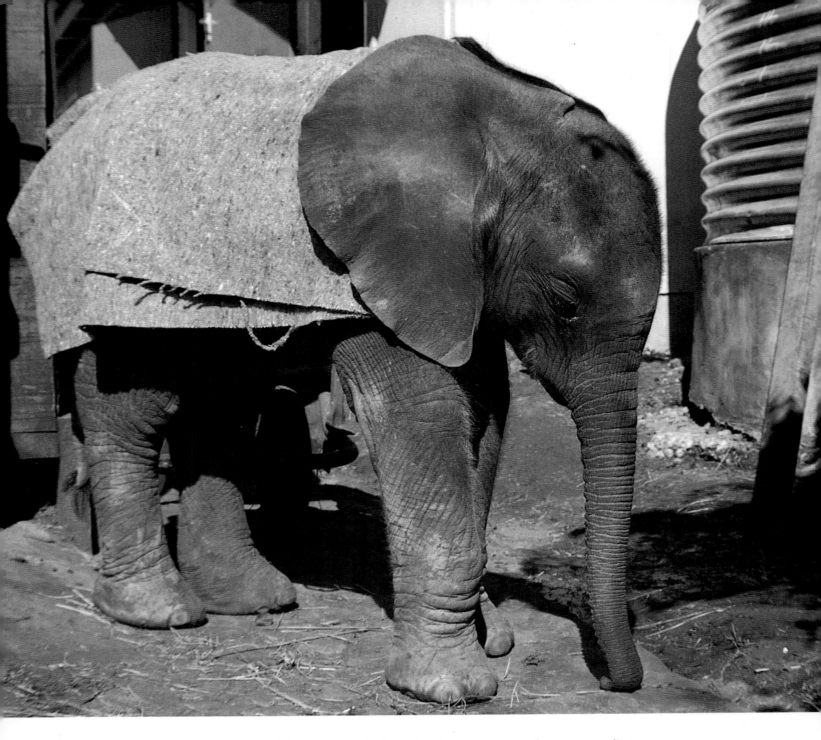

Dika took four months before showing any signs of wanting to live.

After all, up until now he had been the smallest and had enjoyed the extra attention and love. Suddenly, there weren't as many keepers with him and he begrudged the new orphans all the attention they seemed to be getting. He threw some wild temper tantrums. He started to bully, rushing first at Ndume then at Malaika, knocking them as hard as he possibly could, back and forth, until we had to intervene and install some discipline. Elephants are very intelligent and learn extremely quickly. To teach them can be as simple as a change in tone of voice—a strong reprimand—but, just like children, they usually have to hear it more than once!

I found it amazing to think back five months to Dika's arrival. He came from Tsavo and was named in memory of ten elephants, six adults and four calves, that were gunned down on Dika Plains in their desperate attempt to flee. I saw these ten myself and I can never erase those images from my mind—a tiny tail, a trunk, a pile of tiny bones. . . . I had driven down to collect Dika in Jill's small red Renault 5. With the back seat folded down there was plenty of standing room, and he had enough space to lie down, too. I'll never forget that journey as we travelled through the night. For a good part of it he stood with his little trunk down inside my shirt, the warmth of my back perhaps affording him a bit of comfort. From time to time, his soft, gentle trunk would find its way around to my face and he'd gently feel my eye or ear or neck.

It took him four months to show any signs of wanting to live. He wandered around every day so slowly, his head down, eyes down, trunk barely moving, in such deep sadness. On top of it all, he started teething and baby elephants suffer terribly from this. I never ever thought he'd pull through. I must have asked Jill a thousand times for the assurance she couldn't possibly give me. But here he was now, such a different character to the one of those months not long gone by.

Dika stoops for a drink – baby elephants do this before they learn how to use their trunks.

Hopefully, it wouldn't take as long for Malaika and Ndume to find this joy and love for life that Dika most definitely had.

As he returned to the bush, the hunt would be on to find thin, spiky, light elephant-type sticks that a wiggly trunk could play with, a ball, an inflated tube, anything to help Malaika and Ndume forget and eradicate the memory of their horrendous ordeal.

Kioko tries to interest the two orphans.

CHAPTER THREE

As time slipped by the orphans' interest grew. We slowly increased the length of their walks and the time they spent with the others. Their little trunks became more adept every day, and although they still had to suffer the teething process, their trunks started experimenting, trying to latch onto a leaf or stem, trying to pull grasses up, forever inquisitive. Ndume was developing his thoughtful chewing look.

Out in the forest, Ndume was, for the most part, glued to Olmeg. Part of the keepers' work was to encourage them to show an interest in the 'greens', as was the case with Dika. He had become incredibly lazy about doing anything for himself and enjoyed his bottle a lot more than the effort of foraging. In the wild they learn what to eat by pushing their trunks into older elephants' mouths, thus sampling the vegetation. On their walks back to the house for their bottles Malaika would always lead the way—she could never get back quickly enough—followed by Dika, and then Ndume, who had obviously endeared himself to Dika, too. It became very clear that if Olmeg wasn't around, then Dika was next best and he and Ndume became fast friends. Dika was now taking a certain pride in being the biggest of the littles.

The keepers' relationships continued to strengthen. The elephants definitely had firm favourites, which was something we watched very carefully. Becoming attached to one person meant they would pine and wouldn't feed when another took over, so we had to rotate our crew. Until we were confident our new personnel were completely reliable, our main team was on call twenty-four hours a day, something they never complained about. One mistake with a baby elephant can be fatal and for the first year one is walking a tight-rope, the line so finely balanced between success and death.

Out in the forest, Ndume was, for the most part, glued to Olmeg.

Mishak entices a much . . .

. . . happier Malaika onto the tube.

What bliss it can be.

Feeding may look easy, but Ndume and Malaika soon showed us that they had their very particular way of doing so. Their trunks had to settle happily on an eye, ear or mouth, under an armpit or around the neck of a keeper before they were ready to drink. Then the milk had to be the right temperature—too hot or too cold and they refused. Each elephant had their preferences. Jill and I became experts on testing the temperature and a pan of hot water was always carried out to keep those bottles just right. At the beginning they didn't like it if people came to watch them feed. We could stand quietly at a distance, but often we kept well away so as not to interfere during these special and vital moments. The tenderness of expression shown by the keepers was evident, each in harmony with his charge of the day. Also, the elephants knew we were the milk-mixers, and for the first month, if they saw us round a corner, feed time or not, Malaika especially would expect a bottle!

Sam, so tender and compassionate as he meets Malaika for the first time.

FACING: Moments with Malaika and Ndume.

Midday was always a time to look forward to. All the orphans would return to the house and have their bottles. Dika would usually finish first and although his 'tent' was a little way off, his roly poly body waddling with grace was intent on finding out exactly what he might be missing. Again, more discipline was needed for Mr Diks, as we affectionately nicknamed him. Finally, he learnt and would come around the back, but still he expected to be distracted. The washing was hung out there and part of the ground was covered in succulent new grass shoots. Dika's trunk seemed to be slow at learning, or perhaps that laziness was creeping in again, but he did have trouble in curling the tip around these tantalizing shoots. We often helped him as he stood patiently waiting. We would pluck a few, which he'd take without hesitation, then almost immediately he'd be ready for the next round.

Then there was the cushion. As Ndume and Malaika finished their bottles, Dika would roll around on it and we hoped that Ndume would see the fun in it and he, too, would have such wonderful games. Dika even learnt to play football, usually preferring to make a sneaky back pass with a great air of confidence and pride.

After the feed they would all tumble down to the mudwallow in front of the house. This would be prepared each day to ensure the soil was soft and part of it wet and deliciously gooey. Apart from being such tremendous fun, it was important, too. Elephants coat their skins with mud at least once a day if they can, as it helps to keep them cool and gives protection from insects. It was also a good way to raise the spirits of the new arrivals and to teach them, too. Initially, Ndume and Malaika just hung around on the outside as everyone played, climbing all over each other and loving it when the keepers rubbed mud all over them. Afterwards followed the delights of a dust-bath, which they resisted, too. The inner tube of a tractor tyre provided lots of fun; something for lying, bouncing, climbing or falling over on. As the others returned to the bush we continued to try and keep Ndume and Malaika occupied and happy. As they improved, the days were filled with ever-increasing happiness and laughter. I often thought how very privileged I was to be there, to experience these moments, to be part of it all. There was so much love and with the beauty of the blue, clear days filled with sunshine, I just prayed that the poaching would stop.

ABOVE AND OVERLEAF:
After their bottles they would all tumble down to the mudwallow. Initially
Ndume and Malaika just hung around on the outside as everyone played.

And then the delights of the dust-bath. Dika was now
taking a certain pride in being the biggest of the littles.

OVERLEAF: Dika, with the gentlest of expression, as he seems to sense Malaika during a sad moment.

As the two orphans improved, so the days were filled with ever-increasing happiness and laughter. Malaika discovers her shadow!

The inner tube of a tractor tyre provided lots of fun; something for lying, bouncing, climbing or sleeping on.

CHAPTER FOUR

Then it happened. Almost a month later, as if in delayed shock, Malaika became very sick. She started to scour badly, go off her milk and the little condition she had gained was rapidly lost. Her bones displayed themselves even more, her eyes no longer sparkled, her little trunk stopped flopping from side to side, her energy drained away. She got worse and worse and worse.

Little is known about elephant diseases. Daphne did discover in Tsavo that antibiotics taken orally destroy their stomach lining. We made it a rule, though, that when new orphans arrived they would automatically get a short, three-day course of injected antibiotics. We hated doing this, for the injections hurt them. After administering the first one, Dieter would have to approach cautiously. It is no myth that an elephant never forgets: their memories are excellent and one introduction to Dieter was enough. Of course, we were there, too, and as they associated us with these injections, it would take them a few days to forgive us.

We hoped that Malaika wouldn't need more jabs, but after a couple of days, it was clear that Dieter had to come round. He told us that if she showed no signs of improving, we would have to try some oral medicine. The trauma of trying to make Malaika swallow the mixture was another factor we had to consider. We left the medicine for another couple of days, but it soon became apparent that the injections were not enough. We gave in—it was the very last resort. Although we added minerals to their milk, we thought that she seemed to be craving them as she tried eating lumps of earth, and unbeknown to us, she was swallowing cement chips, too. These we were to discover along with the scouring.

Almost a month later, as if in delayed shock, Malaika became very sick.

The expanse of country between Amboseli and Tsavo Wes

I had to go off to Tsavo to continue work on a project I had started there. Unlike Nairobi earth, we knew the Tsavo soil to be rich in minerals. Daphne suggested I send some back. She also knew that the baobab pith—also found in Tsavo—has over ninety trace elements in it (as well as a great deal of moisture and that elephants dig out the bark of this wonderful tree during drought). Finally, calves eat the dung of older elephants, which forms the stomach flora for a diet of greens. So off John and I set.

Two hundred or so kilometres south-east from Nairobi on the way to the coast start the boundaries of Tsavo National Park. The well potholed tarmac road is the dividing line for Tsavo East and Tsavo West. The Park covers an area of 21,500 square kilometres. Tsavo West's headquarters is at the 250 kilometre mark. Tsavo East's is another 100 kilometres further on. This vast area is elephant country—it always has been. I remember as

...which used to be a migratory route for the vast herds of old.

a child, when the road was still dirt, the trip to the sea always filled me with much excitement. Apart from the fun of reaching the coast, the journey was always unpredictable, especially if there had been rain. There was, however, one predictable factor—we would *always* see elephants. This varied countryside of breathtaking beauty is almost unchanged today, but to see an elephant on this same stretch of road is now a rarity.

I knew before I left which tree I wanted to take the pith from—I had often looked at this tree, stopped beside it on the way to Tsavo. It is an old tree, three hundred years or more, and I felt it was filled with wisdom and goodness. I hated listening to the noise as John struck it to take the precious bark, but it was for such a crucial reason. A few months later, I checked to see if its wounds had healed: there was no evidence that we had ever touched it, it was as if this old tree understood.

Eight kilometres after leaving the tarmac at Voi is the East's headquarters and the home of Eleanor, a thirty-year-old elephant, orphaned herself at two years old and now self-appointed matriarch to a small group in Tsavo. Eleanor is truly remarkable. She has chosen not to sever her ties with humans, possibly because at the time she was ready to leave, she was mothering Bukanezi, a young bull who subsequently has returned to the wild. With Eleanor is Mary, now eleven years old. She was destined for an American zoo until Daphne intervened and finally persuaded her 'owner' to let Mary join Eleanor. She was in terrible condition when she arrived, having spent the first part of her life caged, standing on concrete. Her bones were bowed and the soles of her feet were in an awful state. The pads seemed to have separated, leaving two layers of skin, one protruding much further than the actual size of her feet. She must have suffered enormously. It is only within the last two years that she has transformed. Her bones have finally straightened, her feet are healed and her expression has changed.

She became happier and started really enjoying life, especially at the mudwallow. She showed herself to be a complete water baby: always the first in and the last out, splashing her way out and then running around trumpeting, plucking part of a bush and throwing it up in the air as she runs around in circles. Sometimes she comes sloshing her way back in to the wallow for a second round.

Then there is Lissa. A victim of poaching, she arrived from southern Tsavo at approximately eighteen months old in January 1988. I never thought she would make it—she was quite literally at death's door. Lissa is most definitely Eleanor's adopted calf now and they are inseparable. After Lissa, there was Chuma, arriving in November 1988, found about thirty kilometres from the headquarters, another victim of poaching. He collapsed on arrival from severe dehydration. Having picked up Dika two days before, I returned to see what we could do to help Chuma. I took along a basket of oranges to try and give him some vitamin C and nourishment. If there is one thing Eleanor can't resist it is oranges. I started cutting them into segments for Chuma fully expecting Eleanor to help herself. She never touched one piece as I slowly gave them to him. There was no doubt she knew exactly what we were trying to do and she stood patiently next to Chuma as he ate. For a short time after Chuma's arrival Eleanor gave him all her attention, she never left his side. It was most touching. As soon as he was obviously recovering, Mary took over the nannying and Eleanor resumed her role with Lissa, who had become jealous of Eleanor's distraction.

Eleanor and her family, Lissa, Chuma and Mary.

Such excitement and delight on reaching a water-hole.

Every day the elephants go into the bush with the keepers who keep an eye on them, particularly the newcomers who are on bottles, which are fed to them out there. Each evening they return to their stockades, which, after a cool drink, they go into without any persuasion. Lissa and Eleanor share one pen, Mary and Chuma are next-door. However, they are totally free in making this choice, and sometimes Eleanor takes her group off with the wild elephants and stays out for days, sometimes weeks, before returning. Of course, the minute they show an interest in the wild herds, the keepers remain behind and do not interfere with this contact.

Eleanor wallows with immense grace and joy.

We try, whenever possible, to give the new orphans to Eleanor straightaway, particularly if they are strong and over a year old, enabling our keepers to feed them their bottles in the bush. The temperature of the milk is no longer important and being with more of their kind is definitely the quickest road to recovery. To avoid interruption and minimize any risk, our Nairobi orphans do not join Eleanor until we wean them at two years of age.

There are many incredible stories about Eleanor and the following I find truly extraordinary. Just inside the Park is Simon Trevor's house. Until a few years ago, Eleanor would visit Simon regularly, insisting on turning on the taps, but forgetting to turn them off again! She would amble up to greet Simon and drink. One day, there were about ten people standing on his verandah. On this particular occasion, as she approached from fifty yards or so away, she visibly quickened her pace, and with her trunk out in the scenting mode, she hurried to the awaiting group. Without hesitation she went straight up to one lady standing with her hands behind her back, and probed her wrist, withdrawing her trunk a few seconds later. This lady was wearing an ivory bracelet. . . .

But back to the urgent matters at hand. After collecting the baobab bark we had to dig the red soil, so typical of Tsavo, in a place near the river where the elephants frequently stop. Then we waited for Eleanor to reach the stockades at nightfall, and fresh dung was soon collected. I put John on the bus that night with the most curious assortment of luggage. It struck me that had anybody enquired, John would have had great trouble explaining the unusual contents!

For once in my life I was glad of 'progress'. The Voi Safari Lodge, situated close to the headquarters, had a telephone. Every evening I would call Jill, dreading what I might hear. Although she told me Malaika loved the soil (as did the giraffe and other animals that came up to the house), which was moistened and rolled into small balls for her to eat, and the boiled pith, which was included in the little milk that she drank, along with rice-water, she continued sliding downhill and reached rock-bottom. Jill's news didn't get any better. She sounded most despondent, I felt sure I would never see Malaika again.

Eleanor so majestic – towering over Chuma.

For a while, after Chuma's arrival, Eleanor never left his side,
giving him the continual reassurance he so badly needed.

I sat under the Tsavo sky that night, ever brilliant with its billions of stars, and watched a wild herd quietly come up to the water-hole twenty yards in front of me. I watched the cows forever reassuring their calves; I listened to the gentlest of rumbles and then the satisfying of thirsts. They were so gentle, so magnificent that I could not help but think of our orphans in Nairobi and how they should be here. I thought of little Ndume and Malaika, and the future of them all, and I felt overwhelmed by a deep sadness which completely clouded over my heart.

One of Tsavo's many beautiful baobabs.

CHAPTER FIVE

Atanash with Malaika. She constantly wanted a
finger to suckle on or a body to nestle up against.

As Ndume plays, Peter watches Malaika, her zest for life had drained away.

A few days later, not having spoken to Jill again, I drove back to Nairobi. As I approached the house I tried very hard not to imagine the worst. Losing an elephant is like losing a cherished friend. The moment I saw Jill I knew Malaika was still alive. Miraculously, she had started to show an interest in her bottle again. Naturally, she had become very weak and Jill told me that, along with the cement chips, she had been passing blood and what seemed to be the lining of her bowels. She also told me that the morning after my last call, she and Daphne had felt it was only a matter of hours before Malaika would die. Her sickness had not only taken a physical toll but a mental one, too. She had completely changed. From being so independent, she now wanted comforting and reassuring one hundred per cent of the time. She never left the keepers, constantly wanting a finger to suck on, a body to nestle up to, her trunk needing some warmth to probe against.

Ndume was developing into the happy little elephant he is today. Content to go off and explore a tender shoot, wrap his trunk around it, then pluck it and 'chew' diligently—as long as the others were near by! Both he and Malaika were teething—a time when elephants' appetites are not so good, they go off their bottles it hurts them so, just like any child. Elephants, however, are totally unique in that they grow six sets of molars during their lifetime. Each set consists of four teeth, one on each side of the upper and lower jaws. They only ever use two sets at any one time. As each set grows bigger than the previous one, they move forward and the older set is pushed out completely. The last molars come into use when an elephant is around forty years of age and by the end of its life they are completely ground down, thus no longer enabling them to chew. Females remain with their families until they die. Bulls, however, are loners. It is thought that the reason bull carcasses are often found close to a water-hole is because the ageing male elephant will choose such a spot in order to feed more easily, selecting tender grasses which require little chewing. Tragically, finding a bull nowadays that has died of natural causes is very rare. They are killed for their tusks long before they reach their three score and ten.

As time passed, the midday mudwallow became more and more joyous. All the orphans were participating. Malaika was proving to be a water baby like Mary: she was always the first in and the last out. Spirits were high. A favourite game was climbing on top of each other—a time when our keepers had to keep a close eye. In the wild, help is never far away. If someone should get stuck then an older member of the family will be there, gently raising the infant with the use of her tusks and/if need be her trunk, too. Our crew had to be that 'mother', ready to step in and help. Shifting a baby elephant stuck in the mud is not easy, often requiring two guys or even three to unstick the struggling infant!

Ndume tumbles off Dika as Mishak ensures that no-one gets hurt.

Ndume and Dika without a care in the world.

The mid-day mudwallow became more and more fun.

Then there was their pure joy of just squiggling right down into the wallow and waiting for the warm mud to be rubbed onto their bodies. It was, without any doubt, sheer bliss. I always felt it was as much fun watching as participating. The rhinos couldn't resist either.

Amboseli, a year younger than Sam, arrived when she was three months old. Her mother had been speared and Amboseli stood over the dead body for five days, defending it against the attempted onslaught of vultures and other scavengers. She arrived in terrible condition. Taking to her bottle was not the problem, but Daphne had to be well prepared with a canvas cushion as padding in front of her body, for the minute Amboseli had finished, she would hurl herself at Daphne. For three months she was unapproachable. She couldn't forget what humans had done to her mother. Slowly, slowly she settled down.

As time passed Malaika once again became the
happy little elephant we had got to know so well.

What contentment as the orphans wait for that warm mud to be rubbed over their bodies.

OVERLEAF: Then there was the pure joy of just squiggling right down into it.

Sam, Amboseli, Ndume and Malaika enjoying themselves.

Malaika – Swahili for Angel, and her face is just that.

Sam is as gentle as ever. His tenderness is so apparent and his gentleness so touching for an animal of his size. Although only three years old, he was big, but still had to double his weight and grow approximately another foot! Most people seem to have completely the wrong notion about rhinos – they are aggressive only when provoked. Sam and Amboseli showed intelligence and such love, which was just as wonderful as that demonstrated by the elephants. The two species form unusual friendships when raised together and Sam was especially tolerant with Olmeg and Taru, who continuously wanted to climb onto him, over him, and be right beside him. Taru seemed particularly attached to Sam. One day he was sampling what Sam was eating by pushing his trunk into Sam's mouth. Quite accidentally Sam bit the tip, which required an instant call to Dieter who managed to sew quite a large part back together again. Taru was very brave about all this and certainly held no resentment towards Sam. In fact, it wasn't so long after the incident that Taru was back wanting to sample all over again! As Sam got older, he spent his time further away from the elephants. Who could

Sam shows his gentleness once more as Malaika cheekily 'tests his strength'!

Jackson watches Taru very carefully as it wasn't long before he was 'sampling' all over again!

blame him? He never got a minute's peace as long as he was with them and was never allowed to browse without interruption as there was always someone constantly trying to climb on top of him. Naturally, Amboseli joined Sam. Being younger, she was less confident and needed to be with him. Rhinos don't leave their mothers until they are around six years old, so they both had a long way to go.

After the wallow, it was a dusting with earth and then the inevitable rub against a bush or rock. Sam had his favourite rock, which he never failed to stop at and rub his belly on with much vigour. It will always bear Sam's trademark where it has become so very smooth along the top.

We are often asked if the orphans wander away from the keepers, but they don't. The keepers are the replacement 'herd' for the time being, so, as in the wild, the baby elephants follow their keepers wherever they go.

As Malaika continued to flourish and likewise Ndume, we felt that this time we were on top at last.

Even at the beginning, Olmeg and Taru never allowed Sam a minute's peace.

OVERLEAF: Moments of simply pure happiness.

CHAPTER SIX

The days rolled into months and our spirits were high as we watched the orphans' celebration of life. It's hard to explain how one feels watching these perfect creations—but it is more uplifting than anything else I can think of. Every part of the day was special, but in particular I loved watching them return home in the soft evening light; Malaika at the front, followed by Dika, Ndume, then Olmeg and always last of the elephants was Taru, who took his time, pausing to pluck tasty morsels. He has always been the most independent in the bush, too, feeding a way off from the others. Often we had to call and call him before setting off home, then, quite suddenly, he'd appear behind us in full run, realizing he was just a bit too far behind. Sam and Amboseli were alongside, too, and on reaching the house, everyone would go to their respective stables to have their six o'clock bottles and then get warm and comfy until the next feed.

The atmosphere was filled with exhilaration and the exuberance of life. The rains came and highlighted nature's joy. Keepers and elephants alike donned their rain gear and headed into the glistening forest to discover new legumes and the many other different shrubs and creepers.

A wallow, whatever the weather. Keepers and elephants alike don their rain gear.

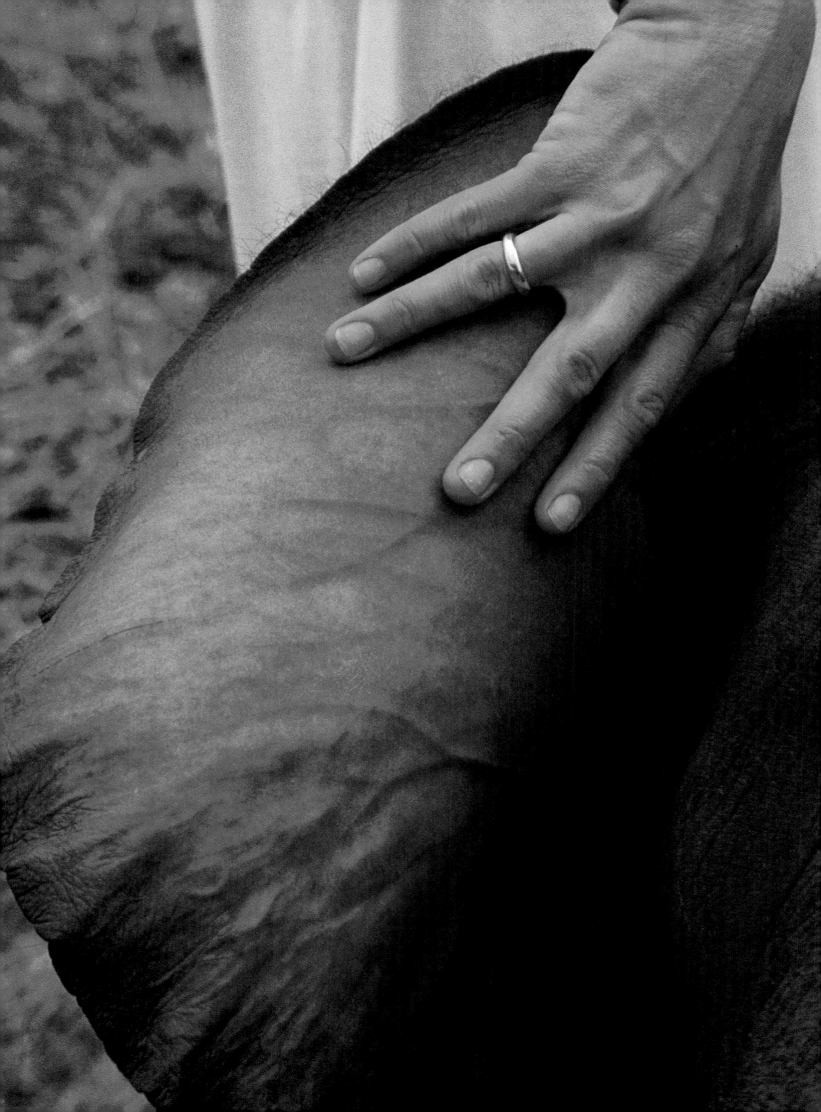

I returned from another working trip in Tsavo the afternoon of 5 July, 1989, to much commotion. We had a new arrival—Segera. He came from a ranch up north under very strange circumstances. He wandered into one of the staff houses at five o'clock in the morning. The ranch hands had heard no noise during the night, which was especially odd as a cow never leaves her calf. It was probably because his family had been killed, but there were no visible signs of his having been left for a long time or having run blindly through the bush. But here he was, pink behind his ears and we knew he could be no more than six weeks old (after this age the pinkness fades away completely). He was frail and desperately unhappy. Yet again we were faced with the same old problems that we had just been through with Ndume and Malaika.

Jill, with the frail, unhappy Segera.

Segera, so pink behind the ears; we knew
he could not be more than six weeks old.

Segera started to show an interest in his bottle, once
we hung a blanket, as with Olmeg and his 'tent'.

Malaika's fat healthy cheeks – she settles her trunk on Atanash's eye or ear, or around Jackson's neck.

Kioko awaits as Malaika decides where she is going to place her trunk.

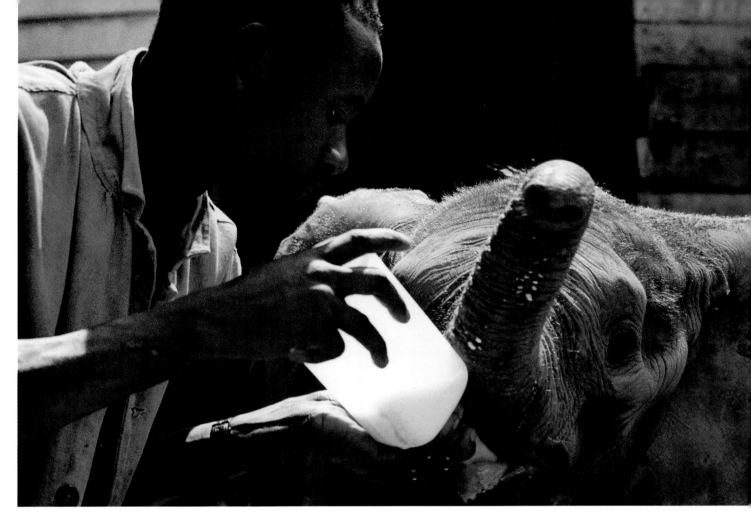

Edo's cheekbones protrude pitifully, unlike those of Malaika.

Edo didn't take long to show what a resilient elephant he would turn out to be.

Malaika and Edo play happily at the wallow.

Something catches Malaika's eye, her ears fan, and off she goes, chasing one of the warthogs.

Edo and Dika.

After Segera came Edo. He differed from the rest in that his mother was not poached. She was found dead in the Amboseli Park by the lodge rubbish dump. She was opened up and inside her stomach were over two hundred bottle tops, plastic bags and chunks of broken glass. All this had been mixed in with the fruit and vegetables that were discarded daily. Edo and his family are well known as the elephants in Amboseli have been studied for many years now. We didn't get him until two weeks after he had lost his mother but he survived by staying close to the swamp, where he could drink plenty of water. He was in very bad condition: his cheek bones protruded pitifully. He seemed destined to die, collapsing after arrival, but when his stable-doors were opened revealing the others, he instantly found a surge of life and the will to live.

Mercifully, the poaching seems to be slowing down. The publicity and pressure are slowly taking effect and people are beginning to listen to the elephants' plight.

But this is not enough. For as long as the ivory ban is not effective worldwide, there will be more orphaned elephants and a serious probability that these intelligent, sensitive and gentle creatures will become extinct in the not too distant future.

Ndume and Malaika with Edo and Dika.

The last paragraph of my mother's book, *African Harvest*, echoes exactly how I feel:

> Yet still we continue, still we refuse to draw back, even though we know the inheritance of which we are dispossessing our grand-children and that it may happen they will one day send up a terrible cry, longing with an unbearable longing to exchange all our mighty progress for one breath of still pure air, for an empty mile and the sound of silence.

CHAPTER SEVEN

Firstly I want to dedicate this chapter to three small elephants that didn't make it—Fiona, Segera and Ol Jori.

FIONA—she was such a gentle, sweet baby—delicate, and so sensitive. She arrived from Tsavo at two months old. After her initial trauma and distress she seemed to be doing well and we had no reason to think she wouldn't pull through. It all happened very quickly. Her 6.00 a.m. and 9.00 a.m. feeds were as usual. Midday she was reluctant, took very little interest in her milk and then lost interest completely. Ten hours later she was dead of pneumonia. John, who was definitely Fiona's favourite, and vice versa, disappeared for two days he was so overcome with grief. He shed many, many tears.

As Fiona sleeps a keeper protects her from the sun.

John, who was Fiona's favourite, and vice versa, disappeared
for two days after she died, he was so overcome with grief.

Dika and Fiona—quiet moments together.

OVERLEAF: A little friend for Fiona as she meets Dika for the first time.

SEGERA—he was such a fragile and vulnerable little elephant. He never got over losing his mother. He never really showed any signs of happiness, but he was improving and had started to go out with the others. During his last week, we had begun to feel optimistic. Then he became listless and as the morning progressed his dung turned an ever-darker red. We called Dieter who gave him several injections, but he died at 9.30 that night from internal haemorrhaging, the cause of which was not apparent. Perhaps the loss of his mother was too much for his heart to bear.

Segera follows Kioko on a quiet walk.

Kioko tests the temperature of Segera's milk before feeding him.

OVERLEAF: Perhaps the loss of his mother was too much for his heart to bear.

OL JORI—Maasai for 'friend', and he was just that. When Taru arrived, Eleanor had got to him before we had time to pick him up. He was three months old and in need of special care. He tried constantly to suckle Eleanor, who, of course, had no milk. We knew if we didn't get him away his death was imminent. Eleanor was so distraught after we finally managed to take Taru from her that we decided to send Ol Jori down to Tsavo to help Eleanor's pain at losing a calf. Ol Jori was thriving—a well-padded, joyful and extremely huggable little elephant, only six months old when we took him to Tsavo. Not long after arrival he showed a certain stiffness in his back legs. I was meeting Jill in Tsavo on my way to the coast. It was obvious Ol Jori needed careful monitoring and as Jill had to get back to Nairobi, I offered to stay and take care of him. He was such wonderful company, but his condition didn't improve. We had Dieter fly down to look at him and as it seemed he hadn't fallen, we thought he must have had a vitamin deficiency. Then we started having to help him move, lifting up his back legs as he walked. A total paralysis set in them. I always knew how bad Ol Jori was when Eleanor returned at night. If she came peacefully up the hill and to the water-hole first before coming to greet him, this was a welcome sign. But if she came up the hill at speed and straight over to Ol Jori, I knew he was in pain. He was so brave: he never complained. About two weeks later, after another of Dieter's visits, I rang Jill. Deep in my heart I knew the worst. Also Eleanor was becoming more distressed by Ol Jori's decline and on several occasions she had tried to lift him—the only time I heard him bellow in obvious agony. Jill and I made the decision to take him back to Nairobi. The usual six hour drive took two days—Jill driving in front of the truck to ensure it didn't go too fast and me in the back with two keepers. A journey neither of us want to remember but one that is impossible to forget.

After a few days in Nairobi, with Ol Jori now incapable of standing, we had to make a decision that was agony—we had to have him put to sleep. The postmortem showed a broken vertebra: a splint of bone had come off and was lodged in a nerve, and he had calcification the size of half a football under the spine. He must have been in the most indescribable pain. It eventually transpired that he had fallen from a rock backwards, landing heavily on his back. No adult elephant was there to avert him from this danger. He left the most enormous void – but ironically, as with all the orphans, he has become 'an ambassador' for the elephants' cause.

He was such a wonderful little friend, but deep in my heart I knew the worst.

I also dedicate this chapter to all the thousands of small orphans who died out there searching for their family, and to all the others, too— babies, teenagers and adults who fell under the fire of machine-guns to satisfy the demands for ivory *hanko* or just so that somebody's whim for an ivory bracelet, necklace, carving or billiard ball could be fulfilled.

EPILOGUE

The last time I found myself on the road down to Tsavo was December 1990 when I travelled as part of a convoy, carrying very precious cargo. It was incredible to think that there we were, Jill driving one vehicle, me another, laden with the most extraordinary supplies, following four baby elephants accompanied by six keepers.

It is nerve racking, to say the least, when you cannot see them, for the trucks are covered, and having pulled over a couple of times before we even reached the main road (a mere ten kilometres) made us extremely anxious.

As it happened there was nothing too serious. Dika destroyed the partition between him and Ndume in minutes and Edo decided the sacks under the seat in front of him were due for inspection. Jill and I probably needed a lot more reassuring than any of the elephants!

As with Taru and Olmeg (who went down in November 1989) arriving in Tsavo was a huge relief, and not just for us either. Seven hours on the road, with the day getting progressively hotter, along with the strange scents manifesting themselves; it must have been overwhelming.

How unique to stand on that Tsavo soil and watch four baby elephants tumble out of the back of two trucks. There we were returning these incredible creatures to where they belong – elephant country.

Back in elephant country.

Nyaga, Dennis, Francis and Peter enjoy watching
the orphans wallow in the rich, red, Tsavo mud.

Sam – as gentle as he has always been.

Sam and Amboseli are returning to the wild in Nairobi National Park. They spend more and more time out there, but every so often they come ambling back for a mudwallow or to spend a night in their pens! It could not be more perfect.

Nyaga, with Sam and Amboseli.

When one gets the bottle – so does the other!

Also remaining in Nairobi is little Ajok, from northern Kenya, a probable victim of poaching. With him is Magwa, a baby zebra found abandoned at a couple of weeks old. Ajok and Magwa are inseparable – she must be the only zebra in the world who thinks she is an elephant!

Ajok and Magwa are inseparable. Mishak and Kioko follow them as they tumble down to the mudwallow.

Magwa must be the only zebra in the world who thinks she is an elephant!

It is with much hope, but with apprehension, too, that we look to the future – a future in which we will hopefully see the orphans uniting with the herds of the wild.